Date Due

Huron Park		
Feb 16/94		
KIR Jul '94		

917
.13541
00222
DeV

92883   De Visser, J.
City light : a
portrait of Toron-
to.

2495

Huron Park		
KIR Jul '94		

92883

917
.13541
00222
DeV

De Visser, John, 1930-
City light : a portrait of Toronto /
[photographs by] John de Visser ; with an
introduction by Rober Fulford and captions
by William Toye.   Toronto : Oxford University
Press, c1983.
1 v. (unpaged) : ill.

1. Toronto (Ont.) - Description - Views.
I. Toye, William, 1926-   II. Title.
019540422X   1812343 NLC

6/he

CITY LIGHT
A PORTRAIT OF
TORONTO

CITY LIGHT
A PORTRAIT OF
TORONTO

John de Visser
with an introduction by Robert Fulford
and captions by William Toye

Toronto
OXFORD UNIVERSITY PRESS
1983

Produced by Roger Boulton
Designed by Fortunato Aglialoro (Studio 2 Graphics)
Printed in Hong Kong by
Everbest Printing Company Limited

Canadian Cataloguing in Publication Data

De Visser, John, 1930–
    City Light: a portrait of Toronto

ISBN 0-19-540422-X

1. Toronto (Ont.) – Description – Views.
I. Toye, William, 1926–   II. Title.

FC3097.37.D48   917.13'541'00222   C83-098051-2
F1059.5.T6843D48

ISBN 0-19-540422-X

1 2 3 4 - 5 4 3 2

To my father, Bas de Visser, who opened my eyes

Foreword

In comparison with most of the other great cities of the modern world Toronto, at first glance, presents a difficult photographic challenge. It doesn't have the rich, historical inheritance of Paris or Athens, nor the pomp and splendor of a royal or papal presence in London or Rome, nor the picturesque setting of Venice or Amsterdam. Yet this very absence of a Forum, an Acropolis or a Grand Canal at once eliminates the need to include such obvious landmarks in a photographic portrait of Toronto. It forces the photographer to concentrate his attention more on the daily life of the city and to exploit to the greatest possible extent the sometimes subtle, sometimes harsh play of light from dawn to dawn.

And Toronto has Light. The light of four distinct seasons. Light, frequently softened by the airs of Lake Ontario, an inland sea, roughly equal in size to all of Holland. Light, bouncing off tall, glass towers to be cast around on streets and other buildings. Light, only briefly reaching down into the city's 'canyons', in each spot at a different and specific time of day.

In practical terms, what this demands of a photographer, especially in summer of course, is to get up very early—when the first faint sign of dawn appears over the Gardiner Expressway and only a solitary car disturbs the silence; when the masts of a hundred sailboats at Bluffers' Park become silhouetted against the eastern sky like some giant armada, and the only activity comes from a family of foxes busily chasing some very sleepy gulls, in a light still too dim for the camera; or when the first commuter train from Oakville comes rumbling into Union Station with the sunlight glancing off a thousand rails.

The photography for a book like this is a process of reaction. Different entirely from the carefully set-up commercial studio or portrait photograph, it is a matter of seeing the play of light, of noticing an arrangement of lines or patterns, or a grouping of people, and sometimes of anticipating a combination or an interaction between any or all of these. Some people differentiate between the two processes as the 'making' and the 'taking' of a photograph. Even if the distinction is not a pejorative one—it usually isn't and it certainly shouldn't be—I agree with Stieglitz as quoted by Arnold Newman: 'The only thing that matters is the finished photograph.'

It is exhilarating to come out of Union Station and find a number of people, each in his or her own space, each in the typical stance of waiting for something or somebody, yet all standing together in a beautiful, spontaneous pattern; or to find Nathan Phillips Square, on a bright, clear day, divided into sharp geometric shapes by a slash of light with just the right number of small figures crisscrossing it to give the scene both life and scale; or to come into the St Lawrence Market very early on a summer morning with the sunlight streaming in through the row of small windows and backlighting the people along one lane of stalls; or to have a few Canada geese slowly glide into perfect position in Humberside Park just as the sun comes up behind the city.

Inevitably the 96 photographs in this book are only a very small portion of the total number taken. The great problem always is which to include and even more which to reject. All of the photographs were taken with Leicaflex cameras, with lenses ranging from 21mm wide angle to 250mm telephoto. The film used was almost all Kodachrome 64, with some Ektachrome.

In the great, complete edition of the Oxford English Dictionary *one of the many definitions of the word 'city' reads as follows: 'In the Dominion of Canada; a municipality of the highest class.' That just about sums it up. To me there is no question about it: Toronto is the municipality of the highest class.*

Toronto, January 1983   JOHN DE VISSER

Introduction

It was a hot summer night on St Clair Avenue West and the street was crowded and noisy. The Italian merchants were having a street fair and they had moved their goods onto the sidewalk. Racks of dresses and boxes of shirts reached out from the stores to the road, and the people had to walk carefully to pick their way through them. About half of the commercial transactions were conducted in Italian, with gestures that a connoisseur might have identified as Sicilian, Calabrian, or Milanese. There were sidewalk cafés serving Italian ices and coffee. At one of them sat an Old Torontonian, toying with the spoon in his *cappuccino*. He surveyed St Clair Avenue thoughtfully.

'You know,' he said to a friend, 'all my life I've wanted to live in a city just like this—a place of the kind you read about in European novels, or see in European movies, where there's variety and public excitement, and you can just stumble on scenes such as this. And now, surprisingly, I *do* live in such a place. But the strangest thing is that I didn't have to move. I just stayed here and it came and surrounded me.'

His experience is common enough. Hundreds of thousands of people, living in Toronto, have watched the city transform itself, by accident and design, over one generation. In this case the phrase Old Torontonian is not used lightly. The population of Toronto changes so fast that in many parts of the city anyone who has lived in one place for ten years is an old-timer; anyone who has been in Toronto for more than twenty has adopted the proudly proprietorial air that, in other places, takes generations to acquire. The Old Torontonian who achieved that moment of epiphany on St Clair Avenue was a real old-timer—he came to Toronto as a baby in 1932. Thus in fifty years he had seen the city through four distinct phases which, like geological strata, define the Toronto experience of his generation.

The first phase was the Great Depression, a time of stasis and quiet desperation, when most Torontonians were interested, first of all, in keeping their jobs—if they had jobs. That Toronto still lingers in the minds of many of us, colouring our response to all the life that followed; today it lives on in the 1930s novels of Morley Callaghan—a narrow, constrained, frightened little city where Christian charity only occasionally emerges. The second phase was wartime, when Toronto was a city of shortages and soldiers, where many people had money (for a change) but few knew what to do with it; 'housing shortage' was the most familiar term in local conversation. The third phase was the post-war period, a time of onrushing prosperity and expansion, when the city gobbled up the farms on three sides of it and covered them with new housing, simultaneously filling its downtown centre with gleaming new towers of steel and glass in which the residents of those suburban houses went to work. This was when Toronto became the financial capital of the empire of Canada and grew as quickly as that empire grew, managing and profiting from the resources which God or nature had left in the hands of Canadians. In that phase immigration played a major part—hundreds of thousands of Italians appeared, for instance, and did much of the construction work—but the immigrants remained in the background. The city's tone was still set by the English, Scots and Irish and their descendants, who had been here for generations. In the fourth phase, however, all that was to change.

The fourth phase, in which we still live, began in the early 1970s. With hindsight we can see that it was announced by two events: the opening of Ontario Place in 1971 and the election of David Crombie as mayor in 1972.

When Premier William Davis opened Ontario Place on the Toronto waterfront his Conservative government signalled the arrival of a new set of social attitudes. Ontario, and particularly Toronto, had traditionally lived by the Puritan ethic. Our public attitudes had seldom been allowed to stray too far from the central tenets of that ethic—hard work and quiet devotion to God. Certainly pleasure was no part of our community spirit, and our strict liquor laws were the enduring symbol of our self-styled righteousness. Ontario Place proclaimed the end of all that. A series of elegant pods set over the water by a German-born architect, Eberhard Zeidler, Ontario Place was and is an unabashed fun palace—a place which mingles rock concerts and children's rides, bars and giant-screen movies, a marina and ballet performances. It's an invitation to the enjoyment of the senses, and in an important way its appearance was the beginning of the Europeanization of Toronto. With Ontario Place, the provincial government and the city confronted the reality of non-Puritan immigrants from southern Europe who brought with them to Canada their desire for communal pleasure. On the Toronto waterfront these newcomers found a high-tech version of the city squares, cafés, and pleasure gardens of Europe; and Old Torontonians found it with them. From the standpoint of traditional, privacy-loving Toronto, Ontario Place was more than a concession to the immigrants. It was a surrender.

That continuing surrender has been the happiest fact of Toronto social life during the last ten years or so. Of course there continues to be racism on the neurotic edges of Toronto society, and of course there must be Torontonians who mourn the disappearance of the quiet, cards-played-close-to-the-vest city in which they grew up. But for the most part Toronto has embraced its new condition—a direct result of Ottawa's liberal immigration policies—with giddy delight. The most visible sign of this delight was the Toronto restaurant boom of the 1970s: in one decade the city changed from a place where the best meals were usually eaten at home to a place where 'restaurant critic' had become a profession. During the 1970s, middle-class Toronto had two favourite topics of conversation: the real-estate boom (which indicated the number of people who were coming to live in central Toronto) and the excellence of the new restaurants (which exemplified the pleasures of the people who were already here). The immigrants were of course the major factor in this change: they owned many of the restaurants and staffed almost all of them.

In doing so, they changed the public tone of society. Torontonians acquired a new veneer of sophistication, and even began—in their exaggerated city pride, which quickly replaced their ancient and also exaggerated inferiority complex—to think of Toronto as 'a great city'. Their pride was fed by outsiders, particularly American, who in thousands of individual visits and a dozen magazine articles began speaking of Toronto as 'the city that works'. Long despised by Canadians as 'Hogtown', and mostly ignored or condescended to by Americans and Europeans, Toronto now found itself desirable and attractive. That was an enchanting moment, and in many ways—despite the economic problems of the early 1980s—it persists.

A year and a half after Ontario Place opened, David Crombie became mayor, a position he was to hold for six years before moving to federal politics. His election was a signal of a quite different kind. Where Ontario Place symbolized the fluid, changing city, the new mayor came to power on a political wave whose basic force was conservative. The reform movement that appeared in the late 1960s and took over City Hall in the 1970s was dedicated, above all, to preservation of the city. Its most vigorous supporters wanted to protect the charming and liveable old districts of Toronto from those who would carelessly destroy them—notably, builders of highways through the city, and property developers who were prepared to raze old streets in order to erect faceless apartment buildings. The reformers were fuelled by love of their own threatened districts and by a kind of Red Tory idealism; surprisingly, they found their most articulate advocate in Jane Jacobs, the great American critic of urban planning, who had moved to Toronto and lived in a district threatened by the Spadina Expressway. In the midst of change and turbulence, Toronto began to value its own past and its own unique architectural qualities. Late-Victorian row houses, streets full of tiny and sometimes eccentric buildings—these had seemed dusty and boring to the post-war generation of the 1950s and 1960s. Now, threatened, they seemed precious.

At City Hall this coalition of sentiment turned into policy. Property developers, nudged by the new administration, began to pay more attention to human scale, and new architectural plans were designed to fit into the existing city. Crombie himself became the symbol of the new Toronto, and his attitudes lingered long after he left office. Today no

Toronto building of historic value is ever destroyed without public outcry, and every old district is approached with nervous care.

In the eyes of someone who has lived through all of these changes—to return to our Old Torontonian, sitting in the café on St Clair Avenue West—the greatest change is not architectural but spiritual. Toronto has developed—possibly as a result of its intense self-regard—something that approaches a collective soul. In the 1970s, their pride awakened, Torontonians became lovers of their city's uniqueness; they became curators who saw Toronto as a kind of living, changing museum; they turned into jealous guardians of whatever excellence they could find or create among themselves. In part this new self-consciousness—which at times shades into narcissism—is the creation of the media, for Toronto is perhaps the most media-drenched city of its size in the world, with three daily newspapers and five local television stations. But it is also more than that. Like any sense of pride worth having, Toronto's is based on experience. Old Torontonians and new tend to like what they have been through in recent decades, and what they made of their experience.

Toronto, January 1983   ROBERT FULFORD

Captions to plates 1–12

1. THE SCARBOROUGH BLUFFS AT DAWN. These picturesque cliffs on the eastern outskirts of Toronto extend for six miles along the shore of Lake Ontario. The first recorded mention of them is in the diary of Mrs Simcoe (1766–1850), wife of the lieutenant-governor, who viewed them from a surveyor's boat in August 1793. They 'appeared so well', she wrote, 'that we talked of building a Summer Residence there and calling it Scarborough'—after the town in Yorkshire, England, with its famous cliffs. The name came to be applied to a village, to the district, and (in modern times) to the borough of which the bluffs are a part.

2. THE GARDINER EXPRESSWAY IN THE MORNING RUSH-HOUR. This expressway, which runs along the lakeshore, was named after Frederick G. Gardiner, the first Chairman of Metropolitan Toronto, a federation of thirteen municipalities that was formed in 1953. The CN Tower on the right, which appears in many of these photographs, is discussed in Plate 18.

3. THE GOODERHAM BUILDING (1892), at Wellington, Church, and Front Streets. Sometimes called the 'Flat-iron' Building because of its triangular shape, the Gooderham Building is seen here in silhouette at sunrise. Behind it are the A.E. Le Page Building (1982), designed to form a backdrop for it, and the two towers of the Royal Bank Plaza (described in Plate 22). These two buildings, and the CN Tower, were all designed by the Webb, Zerafa, Menkes, and Housden Partnership.

4. KING STREET EAST, FROM CHURCH STREET. This area was the centre of the city in the early days. In the background is St Lawrence Hall (1850), a handsome three-storey Neo-Classical building that originally housed shops, a market, and an attractive assembly room on the second floor for concerts, balls, and lectures. Beautifully restored in 1967, St Lawrence Hall still has an assembly room that is available for public use; the rest of the building houses offices and rehearsal halls of the National Ballet of Canada. In the foreground of the photograph is one of the streetcars that first saw service in 1938 and are still a prominent and characteristic feature of the Toronto scene.

5. MURAL PAINTED IN 1980 BY DAVID BESSANT, on the west wall of the Gooderham Building (Plate 3). Painted on panels and incorporating some of the building's rear windows, this work achieves a comically surreal effect by simulating a huge sheet of canvas tacked onto the end wall. It appropriately echoes the theatrical character of the district, in which the St Lawrence Centre and the O'Keefe Centre are located.

6. HUMBERSIDE PARK AT DAWN, looking east from the mouth of the Humber River, with the city lights and the CN Tower in the distance.

7. FRONT ENTRANCE TO THE GRANGE (1817). The Grange was built by D'Arcy Boulton Jr, in the style of a Georgian manor house, on 100 acres that stretched from present-day Queen Street north to Bloor. It remained in the Boulton family for nearly 100 years. In 1875 Mrs W.H. Boulton married Goldwin Smith, for whom changes were made and a library was added. She willed The Grange to the Art Museum of Toronto and it housed the Museum's collection from 1913 to 1918. It is now part of the Art Gallery of Ontario, and was restored in 1973 to represent a gentleman's house of 1835.

8. RAILWAY TRACKS BEHIND UNION STATION, with a Go-Train on the left. Go-Trains (financially supported by the Government of Ontario) provide fast, efficient commuter service between Toronto and towns to the west and east.

9. LOADING AT TORONTO INTERNATIONAL AIRPORT.

10. AVENUE ROAD LOOKING SOUTH. Hazelton Lanes, a large apartment-and-boutique complex, is on the left, and the Park Plaza Hotel is straight ahead. The provincial Parliament Buildings (1893) can be seen in the distance. Even in Toronto it is unusual to take a parrot for a ride in an open car.

11. A QUALITY FAST-FOOD RESTAURANT, Bersani & Carlevale's at Bloor Street West and Bellair. The proliferation of good restaurants throughout Toronto has been one of the most agreeable developments of the past ten years.

12. QUEEN STREET WEST, near Spadina Avenue. This area was once owned by William Warren Baldwin (1775–1844), who gave wide boulevards to this part of the street, which he laid out. In the mid-1970s it was transformed by the appearance of boutiques, bookstores, and restaurants.

1 THE SCARBOROUGH BLUFFS AT DAWN

2 THE GARDINER EXPRESSWAY IN THE MORNING

3 THE GOODERHAM BUILDING (1892)

4 KING STREET EAST, FROM CHURCH STREET

5 MURAL BY DAVID BESSANT

6 HUMBERSIDE PARK AT DAWN

7 FRONT ENTRANCE TO THE GRANGE

8 RAILWAY TRACKS BEHIND UNION STATION

9 LOADING AT TORONTO INTERNATIONAL AIRPORT

10 AVENUE ROAD LOOKING SOUTH

11 RESTAURANT AT BLOOR STREET WEST AND BELLAIR

12 QUEEN STREET WEST, NEAR SPADINA AVENUE

Captions to plates 13–24

13. THE ENOCH TURNER SCHOOLHOUSE (1848), on Trinity Street. Built by a wealthy brewer as a free school, it has been restored for public use. The front part is used by visiting elementary-school classes as a schoolroom of the period; the rest is rented out for various displays and functions.

14. CUMBERLAND STREET. Between Bloor Street West and Yorkville Avenue one block north, Cumberland was part of the Village of Yorkville laid out in 1830 by Joseph Bloor, a brewer, and Sheriff William Botsford Jarvis. The village was annexed to Toronto in 1883. Cumberland and Yorkville are now fashionable streets of boutiques, craft shops, and restaurants.

15. ROSEDALE. North of Bloor Street and east of Yonge, Rosedale has been a residential district since the 1820s, when it was several miles north of York. It took its name from the house of William Botsford Jarvis. In the 1880s it was developed as a select neighbourhood of splendid houses, some of them with large grounds, and for a hundred years since then has symbolized established wealth in the heart of Toronto.

16. TRINITY COLLEGE CHAPEL (1952). Trinity College is a federated college of the University of Toronto, associated with the Anglican Church of Canada. The lyrical Gothic Revival chapel was designed by Sir Giles Gilbert Scott (1880–1960), the most important Gothic Revival architect of the twentieth century, who also designed Liverpool Cathedral and restored the British House of Commons after the Second World War.

17. DETAIL OF MEMORIAL SCREEN, UNIVERSITY OF TORONTO, next to the Soldiers' Tower (1924), and dedicated to students of the University who died in the First World War. The Soldiers' Tower is part of Hart House, which accommodates student recreational and dining facilities.

18. AERIAL VIEW OF THE CITY LOOKING SOUTH. This photograph shows the skyscrapers of the central business core, with the curved towers of the City Hall behind (see Plate 93); the CN Tower; and the proximity to the city of the Island (see Plate 41), with the Island Airport on the right.

The 1,815-foot CN Tower, which opened in June 1976, is the world's highest self-supporting structure (it was built with a continuous pour of concrete) and houses a telecommunications network, a revolving restaurant, and a sight-seeing deck (see Plate 95). It was originally designed to be the centre-piece of Metro Centre—a scheme projected in 1968 that was jointly sponsored by the Canadian Pacific and Canadian National Railways but was defeated in the early seventies. Standing alone—a highly visible and strangely disproportionate feature of the Toronto skyline—it can be seen on a clear day from the mouth of the Niagara River some 26 miles to the south.

19. SUNDECK, WITH JOGGING TRACK, OF THE TORONTO HARBOUR CASTLE HILTON, a hotel on Queen's Quay West.

20. HEMINGWAY'S, A RESTAURANT ON CUMBERLAND STREET.

21. THE EATON CENTRE. See Plate 23.

22. WALKWAY AT HARBOURFRONT. Toronto's own 'national park', this recreational complex was developed on formerly industrial waterfront land and largely financed by the federal government. The Royal York Hotel (1929), a château-style building with Romanesque Revival details, was designed to achieve the monumental symmetry and formality considered appropriate for such a city as Toronto. Until the 1960s the Royal York and the Bank of Commerce (1929–31), two blocks to the northeast, were the most prominent buildings in the Toronto skyline.

Forming a backdrop for the Royal York are the black towers of the Toronto-Dominion Centre (1967–74), designed by Mies van der Rohe (with John B. Parkin Associates and Bregman and Hamann). It is composed of a single-level Banking Pavilion and three towers, the highest of which is the 56-storey Toronto Dominion Bank Tower, which houses an observation gallery. The white tower behind the TD Centre is First Canadian Place (1976), designed by Edward Durrell Stone, with Bregman and Hamann, for the Bank of Montreal. To the right is Commerce Court (1972–74), designed by I.M. Pei as the head office of the Canadian Imperial Bank of Commerce.

The glistening, multi-faceted towers of the Royal Bank Plaza (1976), on the right, appear in many of these photographs (see particularly Plates 3 and 92). The golden effect of the crystalline exterior, which changes as the light and clouds change, is truly gold: genuine bronze-coloured gold leaf was laminated into the glass. Along with the CN Tower (Plate 18), the Royal Bank towers are the most distinctive features in the Toronto skyline.

23. THE EATON CENTRE (1976). Perhaps the best-known modern building in the city, this shopping centre was built by the T. Eaton Company, Canada's old and famous department store. Its most prominent interior feature is a multi-level shopping gallery that runs parallel to Yonge Street. The design, by the Zeidler Partnership, was inspired by the Galleria in Milan and is characterized by airy high-tech industrial detailing.

24. NINETEENTH-CENTURY HOUSES CONVERTED TO COMMERCIAL USE. Facing south on Dundas Street West, these houses—almost all of them built in the late 1870s—are opposite the Art Gallery of Ontario. The building on the left is a prime example of how not to build on a street of old houses.

13 THE ENOCH TURNER SCHOOLHOUSE (1848)

14 CUMBERLAND STREET

15 ROSEDALE

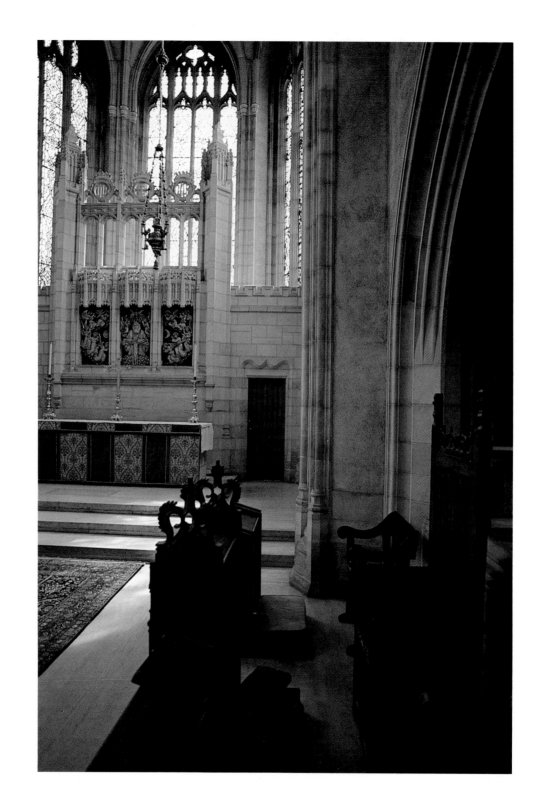

16 TRINITY COLLEGE CHAPEL (1952)

17 DETAIL OF MEMORIAL SCREEN,
UNIVERSITY OF TORONTO

18 AERIAL VIEW LOOKING SOUTH

19 THE TORONTO HARBOUR CASTLE HILTON

20 RESTAURANT ON CUMBERLAND STREET

21 THE EATON CENTRE (1976)

22 WALKWAY AT HARBOURFRONT

23 THE EATON CENTRE

24 DUNDAS STREET WEST

Captions to plates 25–36

25. THE TOWER OF ST ANDREW'S PRESBYTERIAN CHURCH (1876) ACROSS FROM ROY THOMSON HALL (1982). In the nineteenth century this intersection at Simcoe and King Street West was dubbed 'Education, Legislation, Salvation, and Damnation' because it housed the first Upper Canada College (1830), the Governor's residence (1828), St Andrew's Church, and a tavern. Today the Presbyterian sobriety of the church provides an appealing contrast to Toronto's new concert hall (see Plates 57 and 91).

26. LAWRENCE WEST SUBWAY STATION ON THE SPADINA LINE. This, and other stations on the line (which opened in 1976), features artists' decorations that enhance the individual station designs and avoid the sterility that characterizes the earlier lines.

27. A NINETEENTH-CENTURY INDUSTRIAL BUILDING (1888) ON BERKELEY STREET, now the home of the Toronto Free Theatre.

28. OUTDOOR FLEA MARKET AT HARBOURFRONT.

29. OPENING OF ROY THOMSON HALL, 13 September 1982. See Plate 57.

30. TOWER OF ST JAMES' CATHEDRAL, King Street East. There was already a small wooden church on this site in 1807. Enlarged in 1818–19, it was replaced by a stone church in 1833. This burned down in 1839 and was replaced in the same year by a church that was destroyed by fire in 1849. The present Gothic Revival building (by Frederick William Cumberland and Thomas Ridout) was begun in 1850, opened in 1853, and was finally completed in 1874, the year the tower (by Henry Langley) was built. It has been the Anglican cathedral church of Toronto since the 1840s.

31. NINETEENTH-CENTURY WAREHOUSES ON FRONT STREET EAST. Threatened in the 1960s, these grand features of the streetscape were restored in the 1970s and now house shops, restaurants, and offices. The three buildings on the left display rare examples of cast-iron fronts; next to them is the F. & G. Perkins Building (1874), named after a grocery wholesaler; and next to that is the Beardmore Building (1871–3), named after a tanner. These buildings once faced a similar row that was demolished. The space is now occupied by Berczy Park, named after William Berczy (1744–1813), a German painter who lived in York from 1794 to 1805.

32. HEAD OF DIONYSUS, 2nd century A.D., in the Royal Ontario Museum. This is a fragment of one of the many works sculpted for wealthy Romans and based on prototypes from Greek antiquity. The ROM is Canada's largest public museum. The first galleries were built from 1910 to 1913; the wing on Queen's Park Crescent was built in 1933. At present it is undergoing an extensive program of rebuilding and additions, to be completed in 1984. Its collection of ancient Chinese artifacts, much of it gathered in the 1920s and 1930s by George Crofts and William Charles White, Anglican bishop of Honan, is one of the largest and most important of its kind in the western world.

33. MANNEQUIN IN THE WINDOW OF CREED'S STORE, BLOOR STREET WEST.

34. THE CN TOWER, SEEN FROM THE MOUTH OF THE HUMBER RIVER.

35. THE CINESPHERE AT ONTARIO PLACE. This geodesic dome, which houses a film theatre with a screen six storeys high, is part of Ontario Place (1971), a Crown Corporation of the Government of Ontario that was designed by the Zeidler Partnership. It is an innovative leisure complex built on 46 acres of man-made islands interlaced with lagoons and dominated by the Cinesphere.

36. CROSS-COUNTRY SKIING IN WILKET CREEK PARK, DON MILLS. Metropolitan Toronto has a great many parks of different kinds, including small inner-city recreational areas, formal gardens, and ravines that bring a touch of the wilderness, with its flora and fauna, into city life.

25 ST ANDREW'S PRESBYTERIAN CHURCH (1876)
ACROSS FROM ROY THOMSON HALL (1982)

26 LAWRENCE WEST SUBWAY STATION

27 NINETEENTH-CENTURY INDUSTRIAL BUILDING
ON BERKELEY STREET

28 OUTDOOR FLEA MARKET AT HARBOURFRONT

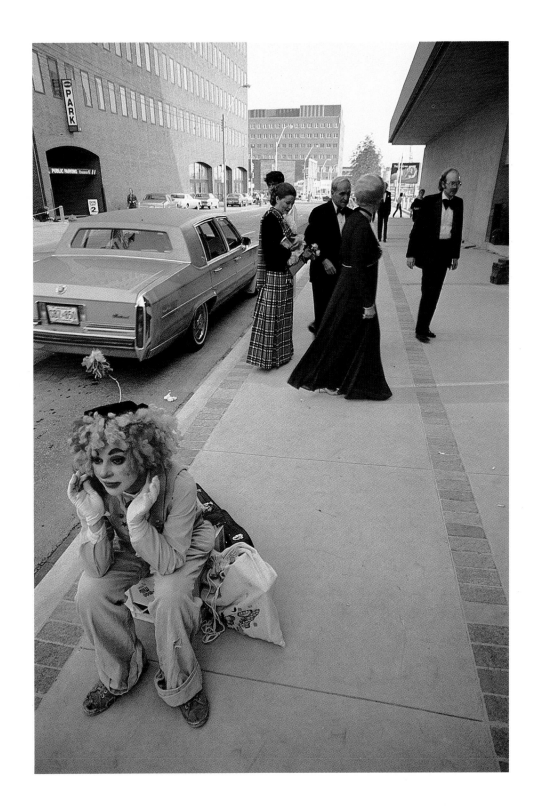

29 OPENING OF ROY THOMSON HALL, 13 SEPTEMBER 1982

30 TOWER OF ST JAMES' CATHEDRAL, KING STREET EAST

31 NINETEENTH-CENTURY WAREHOUSES ON FRONT STREET EAST

32 HEAD OF DIONYSUS, ROYAL ONTARIO MUSEUM

33 IN THE WINDOW OF CREED'S STORE, BLOOR STREET WEST

34 THE CN TOWER SEEN FROM THE MOUTH OF THE HUMBER RIVER

35 THE CINESPHERE AT ONTARIO PLACE

36 WILKET CREEK PARK, DON MILLS

Captions to plates 37-48

37. A RIDING RING IN WILKET CREEK PARK.

38. LAKESHORE BOULEVARD AT NIGHT, looking west, with Ontario Place on the left and the stadium of the Canadian National Exhibition—the largest annual exhibition in the world—on the right.

39. CARIBANA, an annual Caribbean folk festival.

40. KENSINGTON MARKET. This market—which began on Kensington Avenue and spread into several neighbouring streets south of College and west of Spadina—was once predominantly Jewish but is now also Portuguese, Caribbean, and Chinese. A lively and enticing neighbourhood, it features shops for fruit and vegetables, meat and fish, dairy products, baked goods, and even clothing.

41. CENTRE ISLAND. The 'Island'—in reality a small archipelago of several islands—protects the harbour and is a beautiful feature of the city. It was once a peninsula and known as such but in 1858 a storm severed its connection with the city mainland. In the second half of the nineteenth century Centre Island, Hanlan's Point, and Ward's Island became very popular resort areas, with hotels and summer residences. In 1954 the Metropolitan Parks Commission turned the islands into public parkland, leaving only a small, but very distinctive, residential community on Algonquin and Ward's Islands. Although within sight of the downtown core, and only ten minutes away by ferry, the islands offer to over a million and a quarter visitors each summer the refreshing illusion of remoteness, and a sense of rural peace, thanks to the well-kept parks, beaches, lagoons, and woodland paths—unspoiled even by three private yacht clubs, a public marina, and the busy Island Airport. For an aerial view, see Plate 18.

42. KENSINGTON MARKET—a vast variety of grains, peas, and lentils.

43. 'HANGING GARDENS' ON THE BACKS OF HOUSES NORTH OF QUEEN STREET WEST.

44. ENTRANCE TO OSGOODE HALL, Queen Street West. Osgoode Hall houses the Supreme Court of Ontario and the Law Society of Upper Canada. The first building—named after William Osgoode, first Chief Justice of Upper Canada—was constructed in 1829-32. A wing designed by William Warren Baldwin (now the central portion) was added to it in 1833; the present west wing, designed by Henry Bower Lane, was added in 1844-6. In 1857-60 the central portion was rebuilt by Cumberland & Storm in a French Renaissance Revival style that echoes the garden façade of Versailles; the front entrance, with its vermiculated rustication, is shown here.

45. ETCHED WINDOW IN THE MAIN ENTRANCE OF OSGOODE HALL.

46. CASA LOMA AT NIGHT. Recklessly and lavishly piling detail upon detail copied from English castles, Casa Loma (1914) is an architectural fantasy—both an incomparable 'folly' and an endearing curiosity. It was designed by E.J. Lennox for Sir Henry Pellatt, who lived in it for only ten years. It reverted to the city for unpaid taxes in the 1930s and is operated as a tourist attraction by the Kiwanis Club of West Toronto, which rents out portions of it for public use.

47. HMCS HAIDA. This Canadian destroyer, which saw service in the Second World War and the Korean War, is now berthed permanently at Ontario Place, where it is a prominent tourist attraction.

48. BUYING A PAPER, BAY AND WELLINGTON.

37 WILKET CREEK PARK, DON MILLS

38 LAKESHORE BOULEVARD AT NIGHT

39 CARIBANA

40 KENSINGTON MARKET

41 CENTRE ISLAND

42 KENSINGTON MARKET

43 NORTH OF QUEEN STREET WEST

44 ENTRANCE TO OSGOODE HALL

45 ETCHED WINDOW, OSGOODE HALL

46 CASA LOMA AT NIGHT

47 HMCS *HAIDA*

48 BUYING A PAPER, BAY AND WELLINGTON

Captions to plates 49–60

49. THE CN TOWER AND THE TOWERS OF THE ROYAL BANK PLAZA, LOOKING WEST FROM MARKET STREET. See also Plates 18 and 22.

50. THE OLD CITY HALL (1899), seen from the new City Hall. Before it was cleaned in the 1960s the Old City Hall was a dingy building whose soaring black clock tower, facing Bay Street, meant Toronto to generations of citizens. The cleaning revealed the beautiful coloration of the sandstone, quarried near the Credit River; the patterning in shades of pink and beige; and the intricately carved detailing in the upper reaches of the building. It is an impressive Romanesque Revival monument—the high point in the Victorian architecture of Toronto—in which all elements are combined in an organic whole that achieves the rich, picturesque effect the architect, E.J. Lennox, strove for. The affection in which it is held found expression in the public outcry that prevented its demolition in 1960.

51. THE TORONTO-DOMINION CENTRE. See Plate 22.

52. HOUSE IN FOREST HILL VILLAGE. This miniature version of American Neo-Classical architecture is in a residential district, once a separate municipality, whose streets provide serene displays of affluence.

53. CENTRE ISLAND.

54. DUCKS IN HIGH PARK, largest and most famous of the many parks in the centre of Toronto.

55. SUNDAY PAINTERS IN WILKET CREEK PART, DON MILLS.

56. DOOR-KNOCKER AT MACKENZIE HOUSE (c. 1850), Bond Street. This house was presented to William Lyon Mackenzie—the first mayor of Toronto in 1834–5 and instigator of the 1837 Rebellion in Upper Canada—by a committee of friends in 1859, nine years after he had returned to Toronto from exile in the United States. It is now owned by the city and operated as a museum by the Toronto Historical Board.

57. ROY THOMSON HALL, WITH THE ROYAL BANK PLAZA AND THE ROYAL YORK HOTEL. The inverted cupcake form of Roy Thomson Hall (1982), designed by Arthur Erickson, is sheathed with a steel net enclosing square and rectangular mirrors. Both inside and outside it lays claim to being the quintessence of fashionable and spectacular modernism in the architecture of Toronto.
See also Plate 91.

58. THE FOYER OF ROY THOMSON HALL, seen from Simcoe Street through its glass wall.

59. PAPIER-MÂCHÉ SCULPTURES BY JANE BUCKLES, seen through the window of a gallery on Hazelton Avenue.

60. UKRAINIAN DANCERS AT THE CABBAGETOWN COMMUNITY FESTIVAL.

49 LOOKING WEST FROM MARKET STREET

50 THE OLD CITY HALL (1899)

51 THE TORONTO-DOMINION CENTRE

52 HOUSE IN FOREST HILL VILLAGE

53 CENTRE ISLAND

54 DUCKS IN HIGH PARK

55 SUNDAY PAINTERS

56 DOOR-KNOCKER AT MACKENZIE HOUSE (c. 1850)

57 ROY THOMSON HALL, WITH THE ROYAL BANK PLAZA
AND THE ROYAL YORK HOTEL

58 THE FOYER OF ROY THOMSON HALL

59 PAPIER-MÂCHÉ SCULPTURES BY JANE BUCKLES

60 AT THE CABBAGETOWN COMMUNITY FESTIVAL

Captions to plates 61–72

61. ED'S WAREHOUSE ON KING STREET WEST, ACROSS FROM ROY THOMSON HALL. This popular restaurant is owned by Mr Ed Mirvish. He also owns the Royal Alexandra Theatre next door, which he saved from destruction by his timely purchase of the building, and which he restored to its place as the city's best-loved theatre.

62. CANNON AT OLD FORT YORK, cast with the cipher of George III. British troops guarding York (named Toronto in 1834) were garrisoned at Old Fort York, of which the officers' quarters (1816) are still standing. Restored in the 1930s, the fort is operated by the city as a museum.

63. SOLID-NICKEL MODEL IN THE ROTUNDA OF THE PROVINCIAL PARLIAMENT BUILDINGS. It was presented by the Mond Nickel Company to the Ontario Department of Mines in 1927.

64. ST LAWRENCE MARKET. The area of King, Jarvis, Front, and Church Streets was designated for use as a market-place in 1803, and there has been a market there ever since. In 1831 a building was erected on King Street that, after 1834, doubled as a market and town hall. When St Lawrence Hall was built in 1850 (see Plate 4), it too accommodated a market among other facilities; and a new market building was part of its restoration in 1967. Saturday mornings at St Lawrence Market—which extends into a building south of Front Street that was erected around the 1844 City Hall—are among the most beloved occasions in the city's life.

65. A GAME OF BACKGAMMON IN A CAFÉ ON THE DANFORTH, a main artery of Greek and Italian life.

66. FLOWER SELLER, corner of Adelaide and York.

67. BLOOR STREET WEST, at the heart of the city's most affluent shopping district, with the ManuLife Building in the background.

68. A FREIGHTER MOORED FOR THE WINTER IN THE TURNING BASIN OF TORONTO HARBOUR.

69. UNION STATION. Designed by John M. Lyle and Ross & Macdonald, and built mainly in 1915–20, it was opened in August 1927. It is Toronto's most important monument to the early-twentieth-century belief that the railway station, as the symbol of modern progress, deserved the most imposing architectural form possible. Drawing on the grandeur of classical architecture, it was modelled (like many other North American railway stations) on the great baths of the Roman period. Its exterior colonnade, and its immense ticket lobby or Great Hall, created an awe-inspiring environment for the traveller, for whom it was intended to represent the entrance to a great city. Even today, when its transportation role has altered, the Union Station is an impressive 'open gate' to Toronto. It was saved from demolition in the early 1970s when the Metro Centre plan was defeated (see Plate 18).

70. DETAIL OF 'LARGE TWO FORMS' (1966 & 1969), A BRONZE BY HENRY MOORE, ART GALLERY OF ONTARIO. Placed at the corner of McCaul and Dundas Street West, outside the Henry Moore Sculpture Centre of the AGO, this sculpture represents the Henry Moore Collection displayed inside the Gallery—the largest public collection of Moore's work in the world, virtually all of it a gift of the artist.

71. SCARBOROUGH CIVIC CENTRE. Designed by Raymond Moriyama to house the services of the municipal government of Scarborough, it was opened by H.M. the Queen in 1973.

72. MIRRORED GLASS FAÇADE OF MERCEDES-BENZ CANADA LTD, Eglinton Avenue East, reflecting the dwellings across the street.

61 ED'S WAREHOUSE ON KING STREET WEST

62 CANNON AT OLD FORT YORK

63 IN THE ROTUNDA OF
THE PROVINCIAL PARLIAMENT BUILDINGS

64 ST LAWRENCE MARKET

65 ON THE DANFORTH

66 FLOWER SELLER, ADELAIDE AND YORK

67 BLOOR STREET WEST

68 TORONTO HARBOUR

69 UNION STATION

70 OUTSIDE THE ART GALLERY OF ONTARIO

71 SCARBOROUGH CIVIC CENTRE

72 EGLINTON AVENUE EAST

Captions to plates 73–84

73. CENTRE ISLAND.

74. DON VALLEY PARKWAY AT DUSK, LOOKING NORTH TOWARDS YORK MILLS.

75. THE FORUM, ONTARIO PLACE. For half the year this amphitheatre is the setting for performances by many world-famous entertainers, and by the Toronto Symphony Orchestra and the National Ballet of Canada. See also Plate 35.

76. A SAILBOAT IN TORONTO HARBOUR. In the late afternoon and early evening and on weekends from spring until fall, Toronto Harbour is beautifully dotted with sailboats from the yacht clubs and public marinas on the Island and the mainland.

77. THE CITY SKYLINE AT SUNRISE, from the mouth of the Humber River.

78. THE KEW BEACH BOARDWALK, East Toronto, extending from the western edge of Scarborough to Ashbridge's Bay to the east. Badly torn up by winter storms ten years ago, the boardwalk has been renewed to provide a summer and winter playground for thousands of people.

79. HYDRO PLACE (1975), College Street and University Avenue. The home of Ontario Hydro, designed by Ken Cooper, it has a curved mirror sidewall (2,600 panels) and requires no heating plant. Three large thermal reservoirs, comprising the world's largest energy conservation bank, store heat from solar radiation.

80. WIND SURFING EAST OF ASHBRIDGE'S BAY.

81. HOUSES NORTH OF QUEEN STREET WEST, showing the exuberant repainting done by the Portuguese, Italian, and Spanish residents of the neighbourhood.

82. THE ROYAL YORK HOTEL FROM UNION STATION. See Plates 22 and 69.

83. BLOOR STREET EAST NEAR YONGE, looking west.

84. THE BANK OF MONTREAL (1886), at Yonge and Front Streets. Originally the main Toronto branch of the Bank of Montreal, designed by Darling & Curry, this was one of Toronto's most imposing buildings in the late nineteenth century. Indeed, for its flamboyantly romantic carved decorations and its impressive domed banking hall, it remains an outstanding example of nineteenth-century business architecture. It is now closed and its future is uncertain.

73 CENTRE ISLAND

74 DON VALLEY PARKWAY AT DUSK

75 THE FORUM, ONTARIO PLACE

76 SAILING IN TORONTO HARBOUR

77 THE SKYLINE AT SUNRISE

78 KEW BEACH BOARDWALK

79 HYDRO PLACE (1975)

80 WIND SURFING, EAST OF ASHBRIDGE'S BAY

81 HOUSES NORTH OF QUEEN STREET WEST

82 THE ROYAL YORK HOTEL FROM UNION STATION

83 BLOOR STREET EAST

84 THE BANK OF MONTREAL (1886),
YONGE AND FRONT STREETS

Captions to plates 85–96

85. THE DOMINION PUBLIC BUILDING AT NO. 1 FRONT STREET WEST (1929–36). Originally housing customs services and the main Toronto Post Office, this Beaux Arts building adds a note of French elegance to the city in following the curve of Front Street.

86. THE CONSERVATORY, CASA LOMA. See Plate 46.

87. TREES IN FOREST HILL VILLAGE. See Plate 52.

88. CHINATOWN, DUNDAS STREET WEST, an area of fascinating bustle and variety offering everything Chinese from films to foods and pharmacies.

89. IN A FRENCH PAVILION OF CARAVAN. An annual multicultural food and entertainment festival, Caravan is held in the spring in 'pavilions' all over the city and is sponsored by non-commercial ethnic-cultural community organizations.

90. SCULPTURE BY ROLAND EMETT IN THE ONTARIO SCIENCE CENTRE (1969), on Don Mills Road at Eglinton Avenue East. The Science Centre, designed by Raymond Moriyama, is a complex of three interconnected buildings in an 18-acre park on the slopes of the Don Valley. They brilliantly display well over 500 interpretative exhibits of scientific principles and technological achievements, many of them participatory and audio-visual.

91. INTERIOR OF ROY THOMSON HALL. The ceiling of this concert hall is its most dazzling decorative element, having two double rings of lights and suspended chrome lamps and acoustical hardware. The hanging forest of cloth-covered tubes has since been removed. The clear-plastic disks reflect whatever is on the stage—in this case the empty desks of the Toronto Symphony Orchestra. The huge organ above the stage, made by Gabriel Kney of London, Ont., has 5,000 pipes and 71 stops. See also Plate 57.

92. EXTERIOR FACETS OF ONE OF THE TOWERS OF THE ROYAL BANK PLAZA. See also Plate 22.

93. THE CURVED TOWERS OF THE NEW CITY HALL (1965). In this famous building, designed by the Finnish architect Viljo Revell, the curved towers (27 and 20 storeys respectively) flank a domed council chamber that rests on a podium. The City Hall stands on Nathan Phillips Square on Queen Street West, named after the mayor whose enthusiasm contributed greatly to the project in the early days. See also Plate 18.

94. ENTRANCE TO ONE OF THE PAVILIONS, ONTARIO PLACE. See Plate 35.

95. A VIEW, TO THE SOUTH, OF TORONTO'S CENTRAL BUSINESS CORE, from the Observation Deck of the CN Tower. The prominent white skyscraper is First Canadian Place. See also Plates 18 and 22.

96. THE KEW BEACH BOARDWALK, LOOKING SOUTH OVER LAKE ONTARIO.

85 THE DOMINION PUBLIC BUILDING, NO. 1 FRONT STREET WEST (1929–36)

86 THE CONSERVATORY, CASA LOMA

87 TREES IN FOREST HILL VILLAGE

88 CHINATOWN, DUNDAS STREET WEST

89 CARAVAN

90 SCULPTURE BY ROLAND EMETT IN THE ONTARIO SCIENCE CENTRE

91 INTERIOR OF ROY THOMSON HALL

92 A TOWER OF THE ROYAL BANK PLAZA

93 THE NEW CITY HALL (1965)

94 ONTARIO PLACE

95 VIEW FROM THE OBSERVATION DECK, CN TOWER

96 LOOKING SOUTH OVER LAKE ONTARIO